HACKING

A Comprehensive, Step-By-Step Guide to Techniques and Strategies to Learn Ethical Hacking With Practical Examples to Computer Hacking, Wireless Network, Cybersecurity and Penetration Testing

Peter Bradley

© **Copyright 2019 Peter Bradley All rights reserved.**

The contents of this book may not be reproduced, duplicated or transmitted without direct written permission from the author.

Under no circumstances will any legal responsibility or blame be held against the publisher for any reparation, damages, or monetary loss due to the information herein, either directly or indirectly.

Legal Notice:

This book is copyright protected. This is only for personal use. You cannot amend, distribute, sell, use, quote or paraphrase any part of the content within this book without the consent of the author.

Disclaimer Notice:

Please note the information contained within this document is for educational and entertainment purposes only. Every attempt has been made to provide accurate, up to date and complete, reliable information. No warranties of any kind are expressed or implied. Readers acknowledge that the author is not engaging in the rendering of legal, financial, medical or professional advice. The content of this book has been derived from various sources. Please consult a licensed professional before attempting any techniques outlined in this book.

By reading this document, the reader agrees that under no circumstances is the author responsible for any losses, direct or indirect, which are incurred as a result of the use of information contained within this document, including, but not limited to, —errors, omissions, or inaccuracies.

TABLE OF CONTENTS

Introduction 1

Chapter 1: Setting up Your Wireless Lab 3
- Hardware Requirements 3
- Software Requirements 5
- Let's Install Kali 5
- Set Up the Access Point 6
- The Wireless Card 7
- Connection 8

Chapter 2: The Inherent Insecurities of WLAN 11
- WLAN Frames 11
- Management Frames 12
- Control Frames 12
- Data Frames 13
- Sniffing Packets 14
- Viewing Management, Control, and Data Frames 16
- Packet Injection 18
- Important Note 19

Chapter 3: Bypassing WLAN Authentication 21
- Hidden SSIDs 21
- MAC Filters 23
- Open Authentication 25

Shared Key Authentication (SKA) 26

Chapter 4: WLAN Encryption Flaws 31
WLAN Encryption 31
WEP Encryption 32
WPA/WPA2 37
Speeding Up 41
Decrypting WEP and WPA Packets 43
Connection to WEPWPA Networks 44

Chapter 5: Attacking the WLAN Infrastructure 47
Access Point Default Accounts and Credentials 47
Denial of Service 49
Evil Twin and AP MAC Spoofing..............................50
Rogue Access Points..52

Chapter 6: Attacking the Wireless Client 54
Honeypot 54
De-authentication and Disassociation Attacks 57

Chapter 7: Advanced WLAN Attacks....................... 59
MITM...60
Wireless Eavesdropping with MITM........................62
Wireless Session Hijacking 63
Locating the Client Security Configurations............65

Chapter 8: KRACKs... 68
4-Way Handshake KRACK 70

Chapter 9: WPA-Enterprise and RADIUS Attacks..... 75
FreeRADIUS-WPE..75
Security Best Practice..79

Chapter 10: WPS and Probes 80
WPS Attacks 80
Probe Sniffing...83

Bonus Chapter: Staying Safe Online 88
RAT – Remote Access Trojans 88
Web Shells..89
Credential Stealers..89
Lateral Movement Networks.................................90
Obfuscation Tools...90

Conclusion.. 92

Will You Help Me?... 94

Resources... 96

Introduction

Today we live in a digital, wireless world, a connected world and, while this has a ton of benefits, it has its downsides too. Everywhere you go, there are Wi-Fi hotspots and Wi-Fi networks, all making it so easy to connect and do our work or have some fun. Unfortunately, it's also easy for hackers. How often have you read or heard stories about banks, major companies and government institutions being hacked into, all because their network wasn't fully secured? You would think that, as time went on, we would become better at defending ourselves and our data but, instead, it seems that the opposite has happened – the attacks are getting more and more frequent and, frighteningly, far more sophisticated. Why? For two reasons- many people still don't truly understand how to keep their networks secure and the hackers are becoming cleverer.

That's why I decided to write this book. Your Wi-Fi network is the main port of attack on your system and the best way to understand how to secure it is to understand how the hackers get in. You do that by learning penetration testing. I want you to understand what the wireless network insecurities are and how to carry out your own penetration tests on your own systems so that you can find and plug them.

This is a highly practical book and, to that end, you will need several things:

1. Kali Linux – the most popular platform in the world for penetration testing, with pretty much every tool you need for both security and hacking.

2. Two laptops, both with Wi-fi cards built-in.

3. A USB Wi-Fi adaptor

4. Kali Linux

5. Other software and hardware, all detailed in the very first chapter.

As this is the second in a book series, you should already be aware of Kali Linux and have a basic understanding of how a wireless network works, including the 802.11 protocol. We will touch on this though, as we go through the setup of your testing lab.

Chapter 1:

Setting up Your Wireless Lab

Wireless penetration, hacking your own Wi-Fi network, is not something you can do in five minutes. The first thing we are going to do is build ourselves a wireless lab – this is the preparation you need to do before you can dive head-first into real-world testing. This is an almost entirely practical book because that is exactly what wireless penetration testing is. Our lab will help us to try all manner of experiments in a safe environment so get ready to start.

Hardware Requirements

To set up the wireless lab you are going to need the following hardware:

- **Two laptops, both with built-in Wi-Fi cards.** One will be used as the penetration tester and the other as the victim. Most laptops are perfectly fine for this but try to use those that have at least 3 GB RAM – much of what you are going to do is quite memory-intensive

- **A wireless adaptor** – this is optional and will depend on what your built-in Wi-Fi cards are. If they do NOT have support for packet sniffing and packet injection, you'll need an adaptor that does.

- **An access point** – you will need an access8 point with support for the WEP, WPA and WPA2 encryption standards. I'll be using a TP-Link TL-WR841N router.

- **Internet connection** – you will need this for research, software downloads and for some of the tests.

Hi there! If you found the topic or information useful, it would be a great help if you can leave a quick review on Amazon. Thanks a lot!

Software Requirements

You are going to need this software for use throughout the guide:

- **Kali Linux** – download from http://kali.org
- **Windows** – XP through 10, whatever you are using, installed on one laptop which will be the victim

Note

We are using Windows for this, but any of the techniques we will be looking at can be used on any device that is Wi-Fi capable, including tablets and smartphones.

Let's Install Kali

The first step is to get Kali up and running and we'll be doing that on the second laptop, the penetration tester machine. It's easy enough to do; we'll boot Kali as a live DVD and install it on the laptop hard drive.

1. Get yourself a bootable DVD
2. Download Kali and burn it to the DVD
3. Shut your laptop down and then boot it using the DVD
4. From the boot menu, click on Install

This is a pretty straightforward GUI installer so choose the right options for the system on each screen and get the installation started. When prompted, reboot your laptop and take the DVD out.

You will see a login screen; type root as the user name and whatever password you set when you went through the earlier screens. You are now logged into Kali.

Set Up the Access Point

The next step is to set up our access point. Use whatever access point you want; as I said, I'm using the TP-Link TLWR841N router, but the operation and use principles are pretty much the same for all of them.

Let's start by setting it to use OAuth, or Open Authentication and set the SSID as Wireless Lab.

- Turn on your access point and connect it to your laptop with an ethernet cable.

- Open your browser and type in the access point IP address. The default for TP-Link routers is 192.168.1.1 but check the setup guide for yours. If you can't find the IP address, open your command window and type in route – n – look for the gateway IP address and type this into the browser and the access point configuration portal will open.

- Login and have a look through the options; look for those for SSID configuration

- Change the SSID to read Wireless Lab and if necessary, reboot the access point.

- Look for the Wireless Security settings and change to Disable Security, thus setting it to Open Authentication.

- Save all the changes and reboot the access point – it's now running with an SSID of Wireless Lab.

It is important to realize that, by configuring the access point to OAuth, we have set it as the least secure. For now, do NOT connect it to the internet otherwise if there is anyone within radio frequency (RF) range, they can access the internet via your access point.

The Wireless Card

Next is the wireless adaptor and this is a lot easier to do. The wireless card is supported out of the box by Kali and has all the drivers you need for packet sniffing and injection.

The wireless adaptor will be used with the penetration tester laptop:

- Connect the card in a USB port on the laptop and boot it up. Login and open a command window. Type in iwconfig in the console and you should see wlan0 as the interface for the adaptor.

- Type ifconfig wlan0 and the interface will appear; type ifconfig wlan0 again and you will see what the interface's current state is.

Connection

Now we need to use the adaptor to connect to the access point. Ours has the SSID of wireless Lab and has no authentication.

1. First, we need to see which networks the adaptor is detecting. Type iwlist wlan0 scanning in the console and you will see a list of the networks in range. Scroll through the list and you should find Wireless Lab – look in the ESSID field to see the name.

2. Be aware that some access points may share the same SSID so look in the Address field and check that the Mac address matches that of your access point.

3. Now type iwconfig wlan0 essid "Wireless Lab" in the console and then type iwconfig wlan0 to see what the status is. If a successful connection has been made, the Access Point field should give you the Mac address in the iwconfig output

We already know that our access point has got a management interface IP address of 192.168.0.1 What we want to do now is set the IP address in the same subnet so type ifconfig wlan0 192.168.0.1 netmask 255.255.255.0 up at the command in the console and then check that it was successful by typing ifconfig wlan0 and looking at the output.

Now we can ping our access point and we do that by typing ping 192.168.0.1 in the console. Provided your network connection has been properly set up, you will see the responses from your access point. You can also type the arp -a command which will check that the response is from your access point. The Mac address for IP 192.068.0.1 should be the same as the access point Mac address.

Note that you might see that responses to the ICMP (Internet Control Message Protocol) echo request packets have been disabled for recent access points. This tends to be done to ensure that an access point is secure right from the box and only has the minimum amount of configuration settings available. In this case, you could open the browser and get into the web interface to ensure that the connection is running properly.

On the access point, have a look at the connection logs to check for connection. You should see the wi-fi card Mac address making DHCP requests.

Congratulations, you have successfully set up your wireless penetration testing lab. Let's move on to the inherent insecurities of WLAN.

Chapter 2:

The Inherent Insecurities of WLAN

You cannot build anything worthwhile if your foundations are weak and, in the context of wireless networks, if they have inherent weaknesses, you cannot build anything secure on them. By design, WLAN has some insecurities that can be exploited quite easily by packet injection, packet sniffing, packet spoofing, and more and it is these flaws that we will be examining here.

WLAN Frames

As we are looking at wireless security, you should already have a basic understanding of the correct protocols and packet headers. If not, go do a bit more research before coming back here.

Some of the most basic WLAN concepts are those that you should be aware of. To start with, WLAN communication takes place over frames. Three different types of frame are defined in the Type field:

Management Frames

These are responsible for ensuring communication is maintained between the access point and the wireless client. A management frame may have these subtypes:

- Association request
- Association response
- Authentication
- Beacon
- Deauthentication
- Disassociation
- Probe request
- Probe response
- Reassociation request
- Reassociation response

Control Frames

These are responsible for making sure that the data between the access point and the wireless client is properly exchanged and they can have these subtypes:

- **ACK** - Acknowledgement
- **CTS** – Clear to Send
- **RTS** – Request to Send

Data Frames

These are where the data sent via the wireless network is carried and they have no subtypes.

Later on, we'll talk about the security implications of each of these frames when we go over some of the different attacks.

Let's get right down to it and look into how the frames can be sniffed using Wireshark over the wireless network. There are quite a few tools you can use, including tshark, Tcpdump, and Airodump-NG, for sniffing. For the most part, we'll be using Wireshark.

First, a monitor mode interface needs to be created resulting in an interface for the wireless adaptor and this is what we use to read the frames, whether they are being sent to us or to another network. This is known as promiscuous mode in the wired world.

The first thing to do is to set your wireless adaptor so it's on monitor mode.

1. Make sure the wireless adaptor is connected and boot up Kali. Go into the console and type in iwconfig – this will tell you whether or not your card has been correctly detected with the drivers properly loaded.

2. Bring the card up by typing ifconfig wlan0 (where this is the adaptor). In the first line of the

command output, you should see the word UP if the card is running correctly.

3. Placing your card into monitor mode requires you to use a default Kali utility called airmon-ng. Run the utility by typing airmon-ng in the console to make sure it will detect your card – if it does,, you will see either wlan0 or wlan1 in the output line

4. Now type airmon-ng start wlan0. This will create a monitor mode interface that corresponds to the wlan0 computer/device. This interface is named wlan0mon.

5. If you run ifconfig wlan0mon in the console, a new interface named wlan0mon should show up.

Sniffing Packets

Now we can start sniffing packets:

1. Turn on the Wireless Lab access point that you configured earlier

2. Type Wireshark & in the console to start Wireshark

3. Once it is up and running go to Capture>Options

4. Click on Start in the bottom right of the wlan0mon interface and click on Packet Capture

5. Wireshark will start capturing packets and you will see them in the Wireshark window

6. These packets are what Wireshark is sniffing; to see any one of them, click it in the top window and you will see it in the middle one. If you want to see more information, go to the IEEE 802.11 Wireless LAN management frames and click on the triangle.

7. Now have a look through the header fields that are in the packet and see if you can associate them with frame types and the subtypes that we talked about earlier.

Congratulations, that is your first packet sniff completed. If you look at the bottom of the Wireshark screen, you should be able to see how fast the packets get captured and how many.

Wireshark traces can be a little baffling at first. If you are sniffing a network that is reasonably well populated, you could sniff potentially thousands of different packets. As such, it is very important that you learn to find the packets that you really want. You can do this by making use of Wireshark filters – have a play about and see if you can identify the wireless clients and access points that are unique.

Don't worry if you can't do this, we'll be going over it next.

Viewing Management, Control, and Data Frames

Let's look at these filters and how to apply them to look at management, control and those all-important data frames.

1. If you want to see all of the management frames in the captured packets, type wlan.fc.type == 0 in the filter window and press the enter key. If you find the packets scroll too fast for you, just stop the capture

2. If you want to view the control frames, change that filter to read wlan.fc.type == 1

3. And if you want to look at the data frames change it to wlan.fc.type == 2

4. If you want a subtype selected, change the filter to read wlan.fc.subtype and then play about with the different filters. For example, if you wanted to see the beacon frames in the management frames, you would type in this filter – (wlan.fc.type == 0) && (wlan.fc.subtype == 8)

5. Alternatively, just go to the middle window and right-click on any header field and then click on Apply as Filter>Selected. It will be added as a filter, adding the right filter expression you need in the Filter field

Now we're going to sniff the packets for our own network. For now, we'll be looking at those that are not encrypted.

1. Turn on the Wireless Lab access point and leave it configured so it doesn't use encryption.

2. First, we need the channel that Wireless Lab is running on so, open up a terminal and type airodump – ng –bssid <mac> wlan0mon – input the access point Mac address where it says 'Mac.' Leave it to run and you will see the access point on the screen with the channel. Mine says channel 11, yours may say something different

3. To sniff the packets coming to and going from our access point, the wireless card must be locked onto the same channel so run iwconfig,wlan0mon channel 11 (or whatever channel number yours is)

4. Next, run iwconfig wlan0mon to make sure it is correct – if you see Frequency: 2.462 GHz as an output (or something very similar) it is working

5. Now open Wireshark and sniff the wlan0mon interface. Once it has started sniffing, use wlan.bssid == <mac> as a filter for the access point bssid (again, make sure to use the right Mac address).

6. To see the data packets, add this line to the filter – (wlan.bssid == <mac>) && (wlan.fc.type_subtype == 0x20).

7. Open your desktop browser on the client laptop and input the access point URL into the management interface. Data packets are generated and these are what Wireshark captures

Using packet sniffing gives us an easy way to analyze data packets that have no encryption and that is an excellent reason why encryption is so important on wireless networks.

Packet Injection

To do this, we will use another default Kali tool called airplay-ng.

1. To carry out an injection test, open Wireshark and add the filter (wlan.bssid == <mac>) && ! (wlan.fc.type_subtype == 0x08). What this does is ensures that the only packets we see for the lab's network are the non-beacon packets.

2. Now open a terminal and run aireplay-ng -9 -e Wireless Lab-a <mac> wlan0mon

3. Back in Wireshark you should now see a fair few packets on your screen. Some have come form aireplay-ng and others have come from the access point as a response to the packets that were injected.

Important Note

Usually, a WLAN will operate within these three frequency ranges – 2.4 GHz, 3.6 GHz and 4.9/5.0 GHz. However, all three ranges will not be supported on all wireless cards. For example, the older cards may only have support for IEEE 802.11b/g which means they will not be able to operate in the 802.11a/n range. The key takeaway is that you should only sniff or inject packets in a band or frequency that your wireless card supports.

Something else that is interesting is that each band or frequency has several channels so it is important to understand that your card may only be on one of these channels at any one time – you cannot use multiple channels. Think of it as like a radio – there are plenty of channels but the radio can only be tuned to one at a time and, if you want to listen to something new, the channel must be changed. The same applies to WLAN sniffing and this brings us to a conclusion that is also very important – as you cannot sniff all the channels at once, you need to pick the one that is of interest to you. So, if the access point you are sniffing is on channel 1, your card has to be set to channel 1. Abd the same principle applies to packet injection too.

Time to move on and look at how to bypass WLAN authentication.

Found this title interesting or useful? Then a review on Amazon will be highly appreciated!

Chapter 3:

Bypassing WLAN Authentication

Being insecure is one thing; having a false sense of security is something else entirely. This is actually worse because you are not prepared for what happens if and when somebody decides to hack your system.

WLAN authentication schemas are often weak and easily bypassed. We're going to look at those schemas and how we can bypass them.

Hidden SSIDs

Every access point, when in default config mode, sends its SSID inside a beacon frame, thus allowing any client in the vicinity to discover them. When the access point SSID is NOT broadcast, it is hidden and that means that the only clients that can connect are those that already know what the SSID is.

Sadly, this means that many access points are simply not secure, even though network administrators believe they are. A Hidden SSID is NOT a security measure and should never be treated as such.

Let's look at how to find a hidden SSID.

By using Wireshark to monitor the Wireless Lab network bacon frames, we can see exactly what the SSID is.

1. Go into your access point and configure it as a hidden SSID – this option will likely be different across the different access points but, with mine, I needed to go into the Visibility Status option and set it as Invisible.

2. Look at the Wireshark trace and you should spot that the Wireless Lab is no longer visible in the beacon frames in Wireshark. That's what a hidden SSID is all about.

3. To get past the beacon frames, we'll use a passive technique first. This involves waiting for a genuine client to get connected to our access point and, when they do, a probe request is generated, along with probe response packets and these are where you will find the network SSID.

4. An alternative method is to send all stations deauthentication packets on behalf of our Wireless Lab network using aireplay-ng. Type in airplay-ng -0 5 -a <mac> - - ignore-negative wlan0mon. Once again, ensure you use the correct Mac address, that of the router. Two parts of this command need a little more

explanation - -0 is used for choosing the deauthentication attack while 5 is indicating how many deauthentication packets are to be sent. Lastly, -a is specifying which MAC address you are targeting (that of the access point).

5. All of the deauthentication packets from before will now force the proper clients to disconnect and then reconnect. What would be a good idea now is to apply a filter to the deauthentication packets so that we can isolate them and to do that, the filter you apply is wlan.fc.type_subtype == 0x0c

The access point probe response will reveal the hidden SSID and these can be seen on Wireshark. As soon as the real clients reconnect, we use probe requests and probe response frames to see the hidden SSID. You could apply a filter of (wlan.bssid == <the AP MAC>) && ! (wlan.fc.type_subtype == 0x08) which would allow you to monitor any non-beacon packet that goes to the access point and from it. The && signifies the logical AND operator while ! is the logical NOT operator.

MAC Filters

MAC filters are one of the oldest authentication techniques, as well as being used for authorization and are rooted firmly in the wired world. Sadly, this means they are totally unsuitable for the wireless world.

The idea is that the authentication is based on the client MAC address. The filter is a kind of identification code that is assigned to a network interface. An access point or router can check the code and make sure it matches with approved MAC addresses. The network administrator maintains the list of approved MAC addresses and feeds them to the access point.

Let's find out just how easily a MAC filter can be bypassed:

1. First, go into your access point and configure it so it uses MAC filtering.

2. Get the client MAC address from the victim laptop and add it to the filter

3. Once you have enabled MAC filtering, the only address that can be authenticated with the access point is that approved MAC address. If you attempted to connect from a laptop that was not whitelisted you would be blocked and the connection would fail.

What's going on here is that, under the hood, authentication failure messages are being sent from the access point to the client.

So, to beat these MAC filters, we use airodump-ng to look for the MAC addresses of those clients that have a connection to our access point.

4. Use the following command to find those addresses – airodump-ng -c 1- -a –bssid <mac> wlan0mon

5. By using the bssid command, we are only going to monitor the access point that we are interested in. again, a couple of parts of this command are of interest – the -c 10 part is setting the channel to 10, the channel the access point is on, and -a is making sure that the only clients shown in the airodump-ng output client section are those that are connected and associated with an access point, and will display all the relevant MAC addresses.

6. Once we locate a client MAC address which is whitelisted, we can spoof it using another Kali tool – macchanger. Type in this command to do this – macchanger -m <mac> wlano0mon, not forgetting to specify the relevant MAC address. This address will be the spoofed address for our wlan0mon interface.

You should be able to see, if you are following along with this, that once the MAC address has been spoofed we can connect to the access point.

Open Authentication

This is something of a misnomer – open authentication doesn't provide any authentication at all. When access points get configured to use this, what it actually does is authenticates any client that successfully connects to it.

Let's see how to bypass Open Authentication:

1. The first step is in setting the Lab Wireless access point so it uses Open Authentication. On the TP-Link access point, this is done by going into Security Mode and setting it to Disable Security. Check the guide that comes with yours to see how to do it.

2. Next, we use the command, iwconfig wlan0 essid Wireless Lab, to connect to the access point and then verify that the connection was successful

Note that no username, password or any other authentication details were required to get past Open Authentication – see how easy it is?

Shared Key Authentication (SKA)

Shared Key Authentication uses shared secrets, like WEP keys, as a way of authenticating the client. It works like this – the wireless client will send the access point an authentication request. The access point will respond with a challenge and the wireless client has to use the shared key to encrypt that challenge, before returning it to the access point.

The access point decrypts it to make sure it can recover the challenge text it sent in the first place; if it can, the client is successfully authenticated but, if not, an authentication failed message is sent.

So, where is the problem with security here? Well, a hacker could be sniffing the air and listening to the communication passively. They would have access to the challenge in both plain text and in encrypted form. The hacker could then retrieve the keystream using the XOR challenge and could then use the keystream to encrypt challenges sent by this access point in the future – they wouldn't need to know what the key was.

One of the most common forms of the shared authentication is WEP, or Wired Equivalent Privacy. It is one of the easiest to break through and, over time, an untold number of tools have been developed to crack these networks.

What we are going to look at now is how to retrieve both the plain text and the encrypted version of the challenge by sniffing the air, getting the keystream and then use it for authenticating to our access point without having to use the shared key.

This is a bit more challenging than previous exercises.

1. First, set up shared authentication for the Wireless Lab network. For me, it involved going into the settings and finding Security Mode,

setting it as WEP. Then I set Authentication as Shared Key.

2. Now we want a legitimate client connected to the network using the shared key you set up in in the last step.

3. To get past the SKA, we begin by sniffing at the packets that go between our access points and the clients. However, we also want to log the whole shared exchange. Input the command airodump-ng wlan0mon -c 11 –bssid <mac> -w keystream command. We've used a new bit int his command, -w, which is asking airodump-ng to use one file, with a name prefixed with keystream, to store all the packets in. It is good practice to store different packet capture sessions in different files; that way, you can analyze them whenever you want.

4. We have two options – wait until a legitimate client connects or force one to reconnect. We do the latter by using the deauthentication technique from earlier. When a client has connected and we have a successful SKA, the exchange is automatically captured by airodump-ng sniffing the air. When you see WEP in the AUTH column, you know that the capture has been successful.

5. The keystream you captured gets stored in the current directory, in a file that has a keystream

prefix. My file is called keystream-01-00-21-91-D2-8E-25.xor

6. If it doesn't work, use the command, aireplay-ng -4 -h <Connected Device MAC> -a <AP BSSID> wlan0mon. This generates a .xor file. This needs a device connected on the WEP protected target network and will result in packets being generated to spoof the MAC address as a way of identifying the XR stream and the key.

7. To fake the SKA, the command aireplay-ng -1 0 -e "Wireless Lab" -y keystream-01-00-21-91-D2-8E-25.xor – a <mac> -h AA: AA: AA: AA: AA: AA wlan0mon is used. Obviously, your keystream file name will be used along with the correct MAC address. What this command does is uses our newly retrieved keystream and attempts an authentication with the access point that has the SSID of Wireless Lab, along with a MAC address of 01: 21: 91: D2: 8E: 25, as well as making use of an arbitrary client MAC address of AA: AA: AA: AA: AA: AA: AA.

8. Open Wireshark and apply a filter of wlan.addr == AA: AA: AA: AA: AA: AA to sniff the packets. Wireshark can also be used to verify this – the traces will show up on the Wireshark screen. The first packet will be the authentication request that aireplay-ng sent to the access point. The second packet will be the

challenge text sent by the access point and the third packet shows the tool sending the encrypted challenge back to the access point. Because the derived keystream was used by aireplay-ng for the encryption, the authentication is successful and a success message is sent in a fourth packet.

9. Once the authentication has been successful, an association is faked with the access point and this will also be successful. Look in the administrative interface for your access point; under wireless logs you should see a connected wireless client that has a MAC address of AA: AA: AA: AA: AA: AA

Next, we'll look at encryption flaws in WLAN.

Chapter 4:

WLAN Encryption Flaws

Really, it doesn't matter how good your intentions are, the future is never certain and you can't predict it, either. First, we had WEP, designed to be completely foolproof by the WLAN committee. That didn't work out so they moved on to WPA. We all know that both mechanisms have proven unreliable and insecure over time and both have a long history of being hacked, for want of another way of saying it. Time and again, the committee tried to address the flaws and time and again they failed. Right now, although there are no specific public attacks that can currently break WPA generally, there are some attacks that, under specific circumstances, will succeed.

What we're going to look at in this chapter are the difference WLAN schemas and ways that both WEP and WPA encryption can be cracked.

WLAN Encryption

WLANs are responsible for transmitting date OTA, or Over the Air, and, as such, that data must be protected. The best way to do this is through encryption and the following data protection encryptions were formulated by the WLAN committee, otherwise seen as IEEE 802.11:

- **WEP** – Wired Equivalent Privacy
- **WPA** – Wi-Fi Protected Access
- **WPA2** – Wi-Fi Protected Access v2

We'll be looking at these in turn and at some of the attacks that can be made against them.

WEP Encryption

We knew right back in 2000 that WEP was a flawed protocol, but some organizations and some access points still ship with WEP capabilities.

WEP contains many different cryptographic weak points, discovered by KoreK, Martin, Fluhrer, Shamir, Arbaugh, Walker and many more. To understand how to break WEP you don't even need to be able to evaluate it from a cryptographic point of view and in this part we'll be looking at how you can use tools on Kali to break through WEP encryption. We'll be using the whole suite of aircrack-ng tools:

- airmon-ng
- aireplay-ng
- airodump-ng

- aircrack-ng
- and many others

One of the most basic weak points in WEP is the fact that it uses RC4 and has a very short IV value that gets recycled after every 224 frames. This might look like a big number but the chance of an IV value being used four times in 5000 packets stands at 50%. We can take advantage of this and generate vast amounts of traffic, thus increasing the likelihood of reused IVS; this means that we can compare ciphertexts that have been encrypted using the same key and IV.

The first thing we need to do is set WEP up in the test lab so that we can break it.

1. Connect to the Wireless Lab access point and then go to the section in settings for wireless encryption.

2. Set Security mode to WEP. Then you need to set the WEP key length – I set mine as 128 bits, the default key is WEP Key 1 and the hex value was abcdefabcdefabcdefabcdef12 for the key. Set yours how you want.

3. You should now have your access point offering the encryption mechanism of WEP so the next step is to set up the attack laptop.

4. Use the ifconfig wlan0 up command to bring wlano up

5. Now run the airmon-ng start wlan0 command

6. This creates the monitor mode interface of wlan0mon. Type int eh ifconfig command to check that it has been properly created.

7. Now run airodump-ng to find the lab access point and you should see the Wireless Lab running on WEP in the output

8. Right now, we only want to see the packets for the Wireless Lab network so refine the command to read airodump-ng –bssid <Your AP MAC> --channel <the channel number it is running on> --write WEPCrackingDemo wlan0mon

9. The –write flag is used to ask airodump-ng to save the captured packets into a file called pcap

10. Next, the wireless client needs to be connected to the access point and then the WEP key used as abcdefabcdefabcdefabcdef12. When it has connected successfully you should see an airodump-ng report on the screen

11. Try executing ls in the directory you are in now; you should see a list on the screen of all files with the WEPCrackingDemo-* prefix. These are the traffic dump files that airodump-ng has created.

You should notice on the screen that there are not many data packets under #Data. To crack the WEP encryption, we need a whole load of data packets and all of them must be encrypted using the same key so that the protocol weaknesses can be exploited. So, what we need to do is force the network into producing some more of these data packets and that's done using aireplay-ng.

We'll use aireplay-ng to capture the ARP packets from the wireless network and then, to simulate the ARP responses, we'll inject them back to the network. We'll start the aireplay-ng tool in another window and then replay the packets several thousand times – that will result in plenty of traffic being generated on the network. Aireplay-ng has no idea what the WEP key is, but it can still identify which ones are the ARP packets just by looking at the packet size. This is because ARP is classed as a 'fixed header' protocol and the packet size is easy to identify, even in traffic that has been encrypted.

What you need to do know is run aireplay-ng using these options:

1. -3 indicates an ARP replay

2. -b indicates the network bssid

3. -h indicate the MAC addresses being spoofed

Don't forget that you need to add the adaptor that is being used – this is important because replay attacks can only work on MAC addresses that have been authenticated and are associated. You should, in a short time, see the ARP packets that aireplay-ng sniffed and replayed into the network. If you come up against any errors related to channels, go back to your command and append it with this: --ignore-negative-one.

You will also see that airodump-ng has started to register numerous data packets and all of them get stored inside the files with the WEPCrackingDemo-* prefix.

Now we can start cracking!

- Open aircrack-ng using the WEPCrackingDemo-0*.cap option. The aircrack tool will start using the data packets in the specified file to crack the WEP key. It is best practice to use airodump-ng to collect the WEP packets, to have aireplay-ng carry out the replay attacks and leave aircrack-ng to use the packets captured to try cracking the key – and have them all working simultaneously. You can have them all running in separate windows if you want.

- It isn't possible to determine how many packets are needed for cracking the WEP key but expect it to be at least 100,000, possibly many more. If you have a fast network or you are using aireplay-ng, this should take no more than 10 minutes, but you will likely have to restart the entire process a few times.

- Once you have captured sufficient data packets and processed them, aircrack-ng can go ahead and break the WEP key. When it has, you will see the key displayed in the terminal and aircrack will exit.

Do keep in mind that WEP is terribly flawed and, regardless of how complex the WEP key is, aircrack-ng will crack it. All you need to make sure of is that sufficient data packets that have been encrypted using the key are available to aircrack-ng.

Note

It is possible to use the SKA bypass that we looked at earlier to fake the authentication. This is useful if a legitimate client disconnects and ensures that the authentication and association can be spoofed and the replayed packets can be sent to the network.

WPA/WPA2

WPA was the first version of the new mechanism and it mainly makes use of the TKIP or Temporal Key Integrity Protocol algorithm for encryption. TKIP was developed as a way to improve WEP without having to need brand-new hardware for running it. By contrast, WPA2 makes use of the AES-CCMP encryption algorithm, significantly stronger and more powerful than TKIP is.

WPA and WPA2 will allow authentication based on EAP using the RADIUS (Enterprise) servers or a PSK (Pre-Shared Key) schema. WPA or WPA2 authenticated using PSK is open to dictionary attacks. This attack requires just two inputs – a 4-way handshake between the access point and the client and a wordlist containing very common passphrases. Then, with tools like aircrack-ng, we can have a good go at cracking the passphrase.

So, how does WPA/WPA2 PSK work? The per-session key or Pairwise Transient Key (PTK) is derived using PSK plus another five parameters, which are:

- Network SSID
- ANonce (the authenticator nonce)
- SNonce (the supplicant nonce)
- The access point MAC address (authenticator)
- The Wi-Fi client MAC address (supplicant)

All data sent between the client and the access point is then encrypted using the key.

If a hacker were sniffing the air, they could eavesdrop on that and gain all of the parameters with the exception of the PSK. But this is easy enough to replicate – all it is the user-supplied WPA-PSK passphrase and the SSID. These are combined and sent through PBKDF2, or the

Password-Based Key Derivation Function and the output of this is the 256-bit shared key.

In a normal dictionary attack, a sizeable dictionary containing potential passphrases is used together with the attack tool. That tool derives the PSK from every passphrase (must be 256-bit) and uses it with the parameters detailed earlier, thus creating the PTK. This then gets used to verify the MIC or Message Integrity Check in one handshake packet. If a match is found, the passphrase that was guessed is correct. If no match is found, it was wrong and another attempt is made.

In time, if the passphrase is in the dictionary or wordlist used, it will be correctly identified and that is how to crack WPA/WPA2 PSK passwords.

What we are going to do next is crack a WPA PSK wireless network. We use the same steps to crack a WPA2 PSK network that uses CCMP-EAS as well.

1. First, connect to the Wireless Lab access point and set it to use WPA-PSK. Then set the passphrase for it to abcdefgh – this makes it incredibly vulnerable to dictionary attacks.

2. Use the command, airodump-ng –bssid 00:21:91:D2:8E:25 --channel 11 –write WPACrackingDemo wlan0mon, to start the tool and set it capturing the packets and storing them.

3. Now we wait until a client connects to our access point and then we can do one of two

things – capture the 4-way handshake or force the client to reconnect by sending a broadcast deauthentication packet. We'll do the latter as it will make things faster. Once again, if you get a channel error come up, append the command with this: --ignore-negative-one. Be prepared to try more than once.

4. Once the handshake has been captured, you will see a WPA handshake and the BSSID for the access point displayed in the top-right corner of the airodump-ng tool. If you have used the above append on your command, the handshake may be replaced with a fixed channel message. Just keep your eyes peeled for the quick handshake flash; check the working directory and you should see a .cap file generated.

5. Now stop airodump-ng and open the capture file in the Wireshark tool. Have a look at the handshake. Look at the first packet in the trace file – the files with the EAPOL protocol are the handshake packets and you can use the eapol filter to make sure you get them.

Now we can crack the key. We will need a dictionary that contains popular and common passphrases and words. Kali does have several built-in and you can see these in the Metasploit folder. One of the most important things to note is that, as far as cracking goes, you can only be as good as the dictionary you use and the ones in Kali may not be enough. People choose their passwords based on all sorts of things and that includes their country, region, and so on. When you choose dictionaries, take these things into account to give you the best possible shot.

Let's start

1. Open aircrack-ng with an input of the pcap file and a link leading to your chose dictionary file. We're using nmap.lst for this and you will find this in /usr/share/wordlists/

2. aircrack-ng makes use of the dictionary to attempt several combinations of different passphrases to crack the key. If that passphrase is in the dictionary, it will be cracked.

Keep in mind that, because we are using a dictionary attack, the passphrase has got to be in the dictionary that you use in aircrack-ng – if it isn't, the attack cannot succeed.

Speeding Up

So, if the passphrase is in the dictionary, the dictionary attack can't fail. So, what's to stop us from creating one huge dictionary that is full of millions of the most common passphrases and words that we use? This would be incredibly helpful and would increase the success rate of the dictionary attack significantly. There is one issue with that – the time it would take.

With the PSK using a PSK passphrase, together with the SSID, and going through PBKDF2 takes a great deal of time and CPU. The function takes the combination of both and hashes it almost 5000 times before the 256-bit PSK is output.

Next, we use the keys and the parameters from the handshake and verify them against the MIC that is in the handshake. This doesn't take much in computational terms and the parameters are going to vary each time – that means we simply can't work out the computational expense of this step in advance. So, to speed things up, the PSK needs to be calculated from the passphrase as quickly as we possibly can.

What we can do is precalculate our PSK, which is also known as the Pairwise Master Key or PMK. Note that, because we use the SSID for calculating the PMK, if we use the same passphrase and another SSID, we get another PMK – this tells us that the PMK is dependent on the SSID and passphrase.

We're going to look at how the PMK can be precalculated and then use it to crack the WPA/WPA2 PSK.

1. Use the command, genpmk -f <chosen wordlist> -d PMK-Wireless-Lab -s "Wireless Lab" to precalculate our PMK using a specified word list and SSID in the genpmk tool. This will result in the PMK-Wireless-Lab file being created and it will contain the PMK we just generated.

2. Next, a WPA-PSK network is created using the passphrase of abcdefgh (this is in our chosen dictionary) and then a WP handshake is captured for the network.

3. The next step is to use Cowpatty for cracking the passphrase, using this command: cowpatty -d PMK-Wireless-Lab -s 'Wireless Lab' -r WPACrackingDemo-01.cap

4. It will take just over 7 seconds for the key to be cracked using Cowpatty. Once done, use aircrack-ng to do the same attack – it will take more than 20 minutes, showing you how much time can gain by precalculating the PMK.

Decrypting WEP and WPA Packets

So far, we have used a number of techniques to crack the keys but what are we doing with all this information? First, we need to decrypt the data packets that we used the keys to capture. What we are going to do now is decrypt those packets in the file that we captured OTA using the cracked keys.

1. We are going to take all the packets we captured earlier in our WEPCrackingDemo-01.cap file and decrypt them and we will use airdecap-ng to do it. Run the command, making sure you use the cracked WEP key from earlier – airdecap-ng -w abcdefabcdefabcdefabcdef12 WEPCrackingDecmo-01.cap

2. We will use tshark to look at the first 10 packets stored in the file so type in tshark -r WEPCrackingDemo-01.cap

3. WPA/WPA2 PSK works the same way as it does with WEP so type in the command, airdecap-ng -p abcdefgh WPACrackingDemo-01.cap -e "Wireless Lab" and see what happens.

Connection to WEPWPA Networks

Once the network key has been successfully cracked, we can make a connection to an authorized network. This is quite a useful thing to do when you are penetration testing as being able to access an authorized network using cracked key is the only proof you need that the network is not secure.

Let's connect to a WEP network first:

1. Use iwconfig to connect as soon as you have the cracked WEP key. We broke that earlier and it is abcdefabcdefabcdefabcdef12.

Now the WPA network. This isn't quite so straightforward because we can't use iwconfig – there is no support for it with the WPA/WPA2 Personal and Enterprise networks. What we need is another tool named wpa_supplicant and to use that we need a new configuration file.

1. To create the file, type the following at the command prompt:

WPA-PSK TKIP

Network={

    ssid="wireless lab"

    key_mgmt=WPA PSK

    proto=WPA

    pairwise=TKIP

    group=TKIP

    psk='abcdefgh'

}

Call the file wpa-supp.conf.

2. Use the command, wpa_supplicant -D wext -I wlan0 -c wpa-supp.conf to invoke wpa_supplicant.

3. The device will now connect to the cracked WPA network and once it has been successful wpa_supplicant displays a message telling you that the connection completed.

4. Now type dhclient3 wlan0 to get a DHCP address off either a WEP or a WPA network.

Now we know how to crack the passwords we'll turn our attention to attacking the WLAN core.

Chapter 5:

Attacking the WLAN Infrastructure

Now we need to turn our attention to the authorized network and look at how we can penetrate it. We'll use some new attack vectors and try to lure clients to connect to us, the attackers.

This infrastructure is what provides all WLAN clients with wireless services. We're going to take a look at some of the attacks that we can carry out.

Access Point Default Accounts and Credentials

The access points are one of the main building blocks of any wireless framework but, despite the vital role they play, they tend to be one of the most neglected parts when it comes to security. What we want to look at here, to start with, is whether the default access point passwords have been changed. Then, we look at whether they are easy to guess if they have been changed and whether we can use a dictionary attack to crack them.

Important Note

As we move on through this book, things are going to get more complex so I have to assume that you have been through the previous chapters thoroughly and are familiar with the tools. The next few chapters will build on what you learned as we move on to more complex attacks.

Let's start.

- Connect to the access point and try to find the HTTP management interface. Log in using the defaults which are usually admin and admin – yours may be different. Now you can see just how easy it was to get into an access point that retains the default credentials. One very important thing you should do is try to get hold of the user manual for your router online – this will give you an invaluable insight into what you deal with while penetration testing, as well as giving you some ideas on other flaws you could look into.

- What we've done is verified that the credentials were never changed; even if they were, they should never be changed to anything that is easily guessed. If a human can guess them, so can a dictionary attack!

Denial of Service

Another kind of attack that WLANs are vulnerable to is the Denial of Service or DoS attacks. There are several ways that these attacks can be done, including disassociation attacks deauthentication attacks and CTS-RTS attacks, along with spectrum jamming or signal interference.

We'll be looking at the deauthentication attack.

- First, configure your Wireless Lab network so it has no encryption and uses Open Authentication. That way, we can use Wireshark to easily see the packets.

- Next, we connect a Windows client and you should see that connection on the airodump-ng screen.

- On the attack machine, we'll run a directed deauthentication attack, using this command – airplay-ng -0 5 -a E8:94:F6:62:1E:8E -c AC:5F:3E:B3:3A:B0 –ignore-negative-one wlan0mon. You should be able to see that the client is immediately disconnected.

- Looking at the traffic in Wireshark, we can see that many deauthentication packets were sent OTA.

- Now we can replicate that attack. We'll send a Broadcast deauthentication packet to the whole of the wireless network on behalf of our access point, which will disconnect every client that is connected. We use this command – aireplay-ng -0 5 -a E8:94:F6:62:1E:8E –ignore-negative-one wlan0mon

Evil Twin and AP MAC Spoofing

The evil twin is one of the most vicious attacks on any WLAN framework. The idea behind it is to an access point neat the WLAN network but this one will be controlled by the attacker and it will show as having an identical SSID as a WLAN network that is properly authorized.

The idea is that some users might accidentally connect to the evil twin network thinking that is an authorized one. Once they have made the connection, the attacker will start a man-in-the-middle attack and relay the traffic as it would have been done, all the while eavesdropping. We'll be looking at man-in-the-middle attacks later though, but it's enough to know that evil twin attacks are normally carried out close to the authorized network in the hope that accidental connections happen.

It is incredibly difficult to detect an evil twin that has an identical MAC address to an authorized point and harder still to stop them happening. We're now going to look at creating one of these evil twins and combine it with MAC spoofing on the access point.

1. Find the BSSID and the ESSID of the access point using airodump-ng – this is what we want the evil twin to emulate

2. Now we can use this and create another access point using this command - airbase-ng –essid <your chosen ssid> -c <channel> <interface>.

3. You will now see the new point on the airodump-ng screen – to see it, open a new window and run it using this command - airodump-ng -c <channel> wlan0mon

4. Next, we spoof the access point ESSID and the MAC address, with this command - airbase-ng –a <router mac> --essid "Wireless Lab" –c 11 wlan0mon

5. Go back to the airodump-ng screen – it is pretty much impossible to see which of the access points is the authorized one – even airodump can't do it, and that is why evil twin attacks can be so very potent.

6. Next, a deauthentication frame is sent to the client, forcing it to disconnect and then attempt to reconnect straight away. The command for this is aireplay-ng -0 5 -a E8:94:F6:62:1E:8E – ignore-negative-one wlan0mon

The signal strength is higher because we are closer to this one and it will connect easily to the evil twin.

Rogue Access Points

Rogue access points are those that are unauthorized but connected to authorized networks. Usually, this access point could be used by a hacker as a backdoor into the system, allowing them to get past every security control you have in place on the network. That includes firewalls, intrusion detection and prevention systems and more – none of these would be able to stop the hacker from gaining access.

In a common scenario, these access points would be set as having no encryption and to Open Authorization and there are two ways to create a rogue.

1. Through the installation on the authorized network of a physical device that will act as the rogue. Have a go at this for yourself as we won't be covering it here.

2. Creating the rogue point in software and then using an authorized local Ethernet network to bridge it. By doing this, just about any computer that is running on the authorized network can function as the rogue AP.

That's what we'll be doing next.

- First, bring the rogue access point up. We use airbase-ng and provide it with the ESSID Rogue, using this command – airbase-ng –essid Rogue -c 8 wlan0mon

- Next, we want the bridge created between the authorized Ethernet interface and the rogue. We need to install the bridge-utils files first, then create the bridge interface and call it Wifi-Bridge. The command for that is: apt-get install bridge-utilsbrctl addbr Wifi-Bridge

- Next, we add the Ethernet to the bridge, along with the at0 virtual interface that airbase-ng created: brctl addif Wifi-Bridge eth0brctl addif Wifi-Bridge at0

- We use the following two commands to bring the interfaces up so we can enable the bridge: ifconfig eth0 0.0.0.0 and upconfig at0 0.0.0.0

- Next, IP forwarding is enabled in the kernel; this is to make sure that the packets get forwarded and the command is: echo 1 > /proc/sys/net/ipv4/ip_forward

That's it, all done. Now, if any wireless client connects to the rogue AP, we will be able to access the authorized network using the bridge we created. To verify this, connect a client to the rogue, and use ifconfig Wifi-Bridge up to bring up the bridge. You should see that the DHCP daemon on the authorized LAN will send an IP address and we can now use this wireless client on the rogue point to have access to any of the hosts on the wired network.

Chapter 6:

Attacking the Wireless Client

Penetration testers spend most of their time focusing on the WLAN framework, giving only a little attention to the wireless client. It is important to note that hackers can get into a system via this client as well as they can through WLAN. So that is what we are going to focus on in this chapter, some of the attacks that target the wireless client, be it a connected one or an unassociated one.

Honeypot

When a wireless client is turned on, for example, your laptop, it probes for the wireless networks it connected to before. These are stored (in Windows) in a PNL or Preferred Network List and, alongside this, the client will also show any other networks in range.

Hackers can do any of these:

- Monitor the network probe silently and then display a rogue access point that shares the ESSID the wireless client wants. This will make the client connect to a fake network on the attacker's machine

- Create rogue access points that share the ESSID of other close networks as a way of persuading the client to connect. These are usually done in public Wi-Fi places such as a café, airport, etc., where a user may be looking for a Wi-Fi connection

- Make use of information to learn the habits and movements of the victim – to be discussed in a later chapter

These kinds of attacks are known as Honeypot attacks or, sometimes, as misassociation attacks because the fake access point is misassociated with the real one.

We're going to do these attacks now.

Previously, we used a client that was connected to our Wireless Lab AP. This time it's different.

1. Switch the client on but do NOT switch on the Wireless Lab AP

2. Run airodump-ng wlan0mon and see what the output is – you should see that the client is listed under Not Associated and is probing for the network in its own profile

3. Run Wireshark and sniff the wlan0mon interface. You should see a lot of irrelevant packets

4. Add a filter so that Wireshark only display those Probe Request packets that come from the client MAC. The filter is (wlan.addr==<your mac> && wlan.fc.subtype==0x04). Now you should only see the relevant packets.

5. The next step is to begin a fake AP for the Wireless Lab network on our hacker machine, using this command: airbase-ng -a <MAC> --essid "Wireless Lab" -c <channel> wlan0mon

6. Give it a minute or two and the client will connect – how easy is that!

Now let's do the same thing but competing with a different router.

1. Again, create a fake AP called Wireless Lab in the same range as the real one

2. Switch the real AP on, ensuring the client can pick it up

3. Set it to channel 13 and let the client detect it and connect – use airodump-ng to verify

4. Use this command to bring the fake AP up: airbase-ng -a E8:94:F6:62:1E:8E –essid "Wireless Lab" -c 13 wlan0mon

5. Our client is still connecting to the genuine AP so, on behalf of this AP, we'll send broadcast deauthentication messages to our client – this will stop the connection: aireplay-ng -0 5 -a E8:94:F6:62:1E:8E   –ignore-negative-one wlan0mon

6. Assuming that the fake AP has a stronger signal than the real AP, the client will connect to the fake

7. Again, verify this by looking at the airbase-ng output.

De-authentication and Disassociation Attacks

We've already seen how de-authentication attacks work as far as the access point goes. Now we'll look at it in terms of the client. We are going to send only the client some deauthentication packets and break the connection between the client and the access point:

1. Start your Wireless Lab access point and keep it so it is running on WEP. This way, we can prove that an access point and the client connection can be attacked even when they are encrypted. Use airodump-ng to verify the access point is running

2. Connect the client to the AP and use airodump-ng to verify it

3. Run aireplay-ng and target the connection to the access point using this command: aireplay-ng 0 5 -a E8:94:F6:62:1E:8E –ignore-negative-one wlan0mon

4. Note that our client is disconnected from the AP and attempts to reconnect. Use Wireshark to verify this

As you can see, even with WEP encryption, a client may be deauthenticated and disconnected and the same can happen with the much stronger WPA/WPA2 , as you will see now:

1. Set the Wireless Lab encryption as WPA and verify it with airodump-ng

2. Connect the client and check it with airodump-ng

3. Run aireplay-ng 0 5 -a E8:94:F6:62:1E:8E –ignore-negative-one wlan0mon to force the client to disconnect

Easy as that.

If you're finding the information valuable so far, please be sure to leave 5-star feedback on Amazon

Chapter 7:

Advanced WLAN Attacks

It's one thing understanding the easy attacks that a hacker can do but what about the more advanced ones? Penetration testing and white hat hacking are all about finding all the ways a hacker can attack and that means the advanced methods too. So, let's look at some of the more advanced attacks and try them out so you can understand how to protect your own system from them.

The main focus here will be on the Man-In-The-Middle attack, otherwise known as MITM. These require more than just basic skills and plenty of practice to be successful so you know that you are dealing with a more advanced and experienced hacker. Then we'll move on and use the MITM as the base to conduct attacks like session hijacking and eavesdropping, somewhat more sophisticated than we've looked at up to now.

MITM

These are one of the strongest attacks that can be made against a WLAN system and there are a number of configurations that may be used. We'll be using the commonest one – the hacker uses wired LAN to connect to the internet and creates a rogue access point on the client card. This will broadcast an SSID that is very close to a local hotspot in range. By accident a user may connect to the AP or, if the signal strength is higher, they may be forced into connecting, but will think that they are connected to the genuine AP. From there, the hacker can now see and forward all traffic from the user transparently, using a bridge that he created between the wireless and the wired interface.

Let's simulate this now

1. The first step to setting up the MITM is in creating a soft access point. We do this on the hacker laptop with airbase-ng and call it mitm. The command to use is: airbase-ng –essid mitm -c 11 wlan0mon. It's worth noting that, when you run airbase-ng, it creates a tap interface called at0, which you could think of as that wired side of our soft mitm access point.

2. Now we need to create the bridge. This is on the hacker laptop and it has a wired interface, eth0, and a wireless interface, at0. These are the commands you need to create this, in order:

brctl addbr mitm-bridge

brctl addif mitm-bridge eth0

brctl addif mitm-bridge at0

ifconfig eth0 0.0.0.0 up

ifconfig at0 0.0.0.0 up

3. An IP address can be assigned to the bridge ad we can use the gateway to check for connection. Note that this can be done with DHCP too. The command needed to assign the IP address to the bridge is ifconfig mitm-bridge 192.168.0.199 up

4. Try to ping the 192.168.0.1 gateway to make sure we have a connection to the network

5. The next step is to enable IP forwarding and we do this in the kernel to ensure that both routing and packet forwarding is properly done. The command to do this is: echo 1 > /proc/sys/net/ipv4/ip_forward

6. Next, we want a wireless client connected to the mitm access point. When we do this, an IP address is automatically supplied over DHCP, which is the wired-side server. The client will get the IP 192.168.1.197 and, to verify the connection, we should ping 192.168.0.1 – you should see a response for the host. You can also go to the hacker machine and look at airbase-ng,

where you will see verification of client connection.

As an aside and an interesting point, at this stage we have total control of all traffic because it is being transferred from the wireless to the wired interface. Open Wireshark and sniff the at0 interface to get verification of this.

Back to it

From the client machine, ping the 192.168.0.1 gateway and look in Wireshark – apply an ICMP display filter and you will see all the packets, even though they are not for us. That is the real power of a MITM attack.

Wireless Eavesdropping with MITM

We've created the setup we need for the MITM so now we'll look at using it for wireless eavesdropping. This whole exercise will now revolve around the fact that the traffic from the victim is now being routed through the hacker's system and, as such, the hacker can eavesdrop, or listen in, on all wireless traffic sent and received on the victim's system.

1. Repeat the setup from earlier and open Wireshark. You should see that, now, the MITM-ridge is being displayed and, if we wanted to, we could also look at the bridge traffic.

2. Start Wireshark sniffing the at0 interface. This will allow us to see all the traffic the sent to and received from the wireless client.

3. Open a webpage on the wireless client and open your AP settings. Because my wireless AP was connected to LAN as well, I used http://192.168.0.1 to open it

4. Do this on yours and sign in with your password – this gets you into the management interface

5. You should now be seeing quite a bit of activity on the Wireshark screen so add an HTTP filter so that we only see the web traffic, nothing else.

6. From there, you should be able to spot the HTTP post request very easily – this is what sent the password to the wireless AP.

Wireless Session Hijacking

Another interesting attack that the MITM setup can be used to facilitate is called application session hijacking. While a MITM attack is ongoing, all data packets from the victim are routed to the hacker and it becomes their responsibility to relay the packets to where they should legitimately go, and then relay responses back to the victim. One thing that is interesting to note is, hackers can make changes to the data in these packets, provided it has not been encrypted or is tamper-proof. This means the hacker can modify the packets, mangle them or even drop them (silently).

We're going to look at how to use the MITM setup to do DNS hijacking over a wireless connection. From there, we'll do a hijack on the browser session.

- Again, set the test up as you did for the MITM attack

- Go to the victim laptop and open the browser; go to https://www.google.com

- Open Wireshark to keep an eye on the traffic

- Apply a DNS filter in Wireshark to we only see the requests from the victim to https://www.google.com

- We want to hijack this browser session so the next step is sending some fake DNS responses. These will result in the IP address (in this case, https://www.google.com) being resolved to the hacker's computer IP address, which is 192.168.0.199. To do this, we use a tool called dnsspoof and this command: dnsspoof -i mitm-bridge

- Refresh the browser and you should see in Wireshark that, when the victim puts in a DNS request for any host, not just https://www.google.com, a response comes from dnsspoof.

- You will see a message on the victim's laptop saying, "Unable to Connect." Why? Because, although the changed the Google IP address to 192.168.0.199, which is that of the hacker, port 80 does not have a listening service.

- We can fix this using Apache, built-in to Kali, so input this command: apachet2ctl start

- Now, when the browser is refreshed again in the victim computer, we get the default Apache page that says, "It Works!".

This shows you how easy it is to hijack a victim session, intercept the data and send back fake responses.

Locating the Client Security Configurations

We looked at creating a Honeypot attack for WEP-encrypted and WPA open access points but, when you are doing your testing, and you spot client probe requests, how do you know the network that the SSID being probed belongs to?

The solution is simpler than you might think. What we do is creates some access points that declare an identical SSID but each having a different security configuration and these are all done simultaneously. When a client is roaming, looking for a network, it will make an automatic connection to one of the APs based on what the stored security configuration is.

Let's do a deauthentication attack.

For the purposes of this exercise, we will assume that the Wireless Lab network has been configured on the wireless client. This will be sending active probe requests for the networks when it has no connection to any AP. To find the network security configuration, we need to create several more access points. Again, we will make the assumption that the wireless client profile is either an open network, has WEP encryption, is WPA-PSK or WPA2-PSK. That means four access points are required.

1. The first step is to create four interfaces, all virtual. They will be wlan0, wlan1. Wlan2, and wlan3 and the command to use for each one is: iw wlan0 interface add wlan0mon type monitor, not forgetting to change the number at the end of the monitor name for each one. Use the iwconfig command to see them all.

2. First, the open AP is created on wlan0mon with this command: airbase-ng –essid "Wireless Lab" -a AA:AA:AA:AA:AA:AA -c 3 wlan0mon

3. Next, the AP with WEP encryption is created on wlan0mon1: airbase-ng –essid "Wireless Lab" -a BB:BB:BB:BB:BB:BB -w 1 wlan0mon1

4. And on wlan0mon2, we create the WPA-PSK access point: airbase-ng -a

CC:CC:CC:CC:CC:CC –essid "Wireless Lab" -N -W 1 -Z 1 -c 3 wlan0mon 2

5. And lastly, the WPA2-PSK access point on wlan0mon3: airbase-ng -a DD:DD:DD:DD:DD:DD –essid "Wireless Lab" -N -W 1 -Z 2 -c 3 wlan0mon3

6. Making sure it is on the same channel, run airodump-ng to make sure that all these APs are running

7. Now we can switch the Wi-Fi on for the roaming client and, depending on what Wireless Lab AP it connected to before, it will try that one again, thus telling us what its security configuration is!

This is a useful technique for finding out the security configurations for penetration testing, simply by baiting the client in a that is also known as WiFishing.

Chapter 8:

KRACKs

Back in 2017, a team from KU Leuven disclosed a series of vulnerabilities, collectively known as KRACK, or Key Reinstallation AttaCKs. A KRACK attack is where a basic flaw in a WPA3 handshake is exploited so that one part of the handshake is resent with the purpose of overwriting cryptographic data.

We are going to talk about the theory behind the attack and give you guidance on how to identify and exploit the vulnerability successfully. This is more advanced so if you are still not sure, go back over the rest of this guide first, before you come back to this chapter.

We'll start by looking at the WPA2 handshake. You can find the standard for this in the official IEEE 802.11 standards. We'll begin after the authentication and association stages as these do not affect the vulnerability.

The PTK, or Pairwise Transient Key, that we use for the encryption, comprises of five attributes:

1. **PMK** – the Pairwise Master Key, which is a shared secret

2. **ANonce** – nonce value that the access point creates

3. **SNonce** – nonce value that the user station creates

4. **APMAC** – MAC address for the access point

5. **STAMAC** – MAC address for the user station

Through the entire process, MIC, or Message Identification Codes, provide a certain level of security and of integrity. However, while these are required for the process to work correctly, they do not get included in the cryptographic data that results from the process.

Right now, one result of the association and authentication process at the start is that both the access point and the user station will have the PMK, the STAMAC and the APMAC. Plus, each stage will also have a KRC, or Key Replay Counter, that tracks the packet order, which comes into the process later on. These are the four stages of the handshake:

- The ANonce value is transmitted by the access point to the user station. This gives the user station all it will need for the PTK to be generated. The PTK is created by the user station and now contains the key that will be used for the encryption.

- The user station will send its own nonce value back, together with a MIC. Now, the access point has all it needs for the PTK. It creates that PTK and is left in the exact same state as the user station is in.

- The GTK, or Group Temporal Key, is created by the access point and sent to the user. The GTK enables non-directed traffic to be read, like broadcast or multicast traffic.

- An acknowledged statement is returned by the user station.

After the handshake, encrypted data can be sent from the user station to the access point, where it will be accepted. Now, the negotiation stage is over and the user station can use the network freely.

4-Way Handshake KRACK

Keeping all of that in mind, does it surprise you that this entire process is open to attack? The issue does not lie with the core concept; rather it is within the standard's implementation in practical terms. Like most of the technical standards of today, there were certain sacrifices made in the solution for the security just to make it user-friendly. The biggest sacrifice made here was that, should a message be missed, certain phases in the handshake were made replayable.

For the most part, this isn't too much of a problem. Where it is a problem is in stage 3. Because this is replayable, it can have a massive effect on the overall security. If an attacker were to put themselves in a MITM attack position while the authentication process is ongoing, they could block the PTK that is negotiated correctly and put their own in. Whenever a key is negotiated, the RPC and the nonce values associated with it are reset so, if specific packets are blocked, a MITM hacker has the ability to predict the counter and the nonce values by forcing a key to reinstall. This opens the way for malicious actions by future attackers, such as spoofing, decryption, and packet replay.

However, to yield to the way the security industry works, their researchers have, so far, only published PoC or Proof of Concept scripts. These show that such an attack could happen on a client device; what they haven't done is released the full scripts of how the attack is carried out on a network that is fully established. It is worth noting that they have said both Linux and Android distributions are more vulnerable to a key reinstall which forces an all-zero key to be used which, in effect, makes the traffic decryption immaterial.

Let's get KRACKing.

We are going to use open-source scripts that come from a GitHub page owned by Mathy VanHoef.

1. Open a Kali terminal and type in: :/# git clone https:/github.com/vanhoefm/krackattacks-scripts

2. We also need the dependencies for this project so type in this command: apt-get install libnl-3-dev libnl-genl-3-dev pkg-config libssl-dev net-tools git sysfsutils python-scapy python-pycryptodome

3. Now go to the krackattacks-scripts directory we just created and look at what's in there. You should see the testing script body and the solution that at Mathy Vanhoef came up with. Before we start messing about those, we need to do something else

4. A hostapd six required in the format that the scripts need so go into the hostapd directory by using these two commands:

:/krackattacks-scripts/hostapd# cp defconfig .config

:/krackattacks-scripts/hostapd# make -j 2

5. What this does is compile hostapd so it can be used in the KRACK PoC scripts. Use the ls command to go into the krackattack directory. The scripts will tell you to execute the script called disable-hwcrypto .sh straight away but, if you have gone down the route of using a virtual machine (although we haven't discussed this), be aware that the VM may crash.

This directory contains three more important files. The first one is called hostapd.conf and this is where the Wi-Fi details are defined for the network that is being generated. The default SSID is testnetwork and the default passphrase is abcdefgh, but you can change these as you wish. The next file is called krack-test-client.py script and this is the one we will use to identify the devices that are vulnerable – this is going to be the main part of this chapter. Lastly, we have krack-ft-test.py – we are NOT going to be discussing that here because its application to niche devices is outside the scope of this book.

Now, we really are going to start KRACKing.

1. The network manager must be disabled so that we don't get any conflicts; use these commands: systemctl stop NetworkManager.servicesystemctl disable NetworkManager.service

2. Next, krack-test-client.py needs to be executed, using this command: python krack-test-client.py

3. Read the screen that appears and then get a test device – you can use any device that has Wi-Fi enabled – and connect it to the network we created. Use the default credentials or the ones you set it to if you changed them

4. You will see the terminal fill up with text, but the script you used will highlight the successes in green

5. The script iterates through all the potential attacks and tells you whether the tested device is vulnerable or not.

Expect this attack to be developed as time goes by and more scripts get released. You should also take a look at the white paper to get a better understanding - https://papers.mathyvanhoef.com/ccs2017.pdf.

Chapter 9:

WPA-Enterprise and RADIUS Attacks

It's always been thought that WPA-Enterprise was unbreakable and many network administrators believe it is the only answer they need to secure their wireless network. What we are going to see in this chapter is how wrong this is.

We are going to look at how we can use Kali to attack WPA-Enterprise and we'll be looking at setting up FreeRADIUS-WPE, how to attack PEAP on Windows, along with some best practices for security.

FreeRADIUS-WPE

To set this up, we require a RADIUS server to carry out the WPA-Enterprise attack. FreeRADIUS is the most commonly used of the open source RADIUS servers. However, it isn't very easy to set up and having to configure it for every attack is time-consuming.

One of the better-known security researchers, Joshua Wright, came up with a patch for the server that makes it a lot easier to set up and use for attacks. It's called

FreeRADIUS-WPE, which stands for Wireless Pwnage Edition, but it doesn't ship with Kali so you need to set it up:

1. Use the command, apt-get install freeradius-wpe to install FreeRADIUS-WPE and then check the output to confirm it's done.

2. Now we'll set up the RADIUS server. Go to your access point and connect a LAN port to the Ethernet port on your Kali machine (eth0, in our case). Bring the interface up and run DHCP to get an IP address running

3. Next, log in to your access point, go to Security mode and set it as WPA/WPA2-Enterprise. Then set Version as WPA2, Encryption as AES and, where it seas EAP (802.1x), input the Radius server IP (this will be the IP address for your kali build) and the password as test.

4. Open a terminal and go to the /etc/freeradius-wpe/3.0 directory. You will find all the configuration files for FreeRADIUS-WPE here.

5. Open /mods-available/eap – the default_eap_type command is md5

6. We want to change it to peap so go to clients.conf. We will be defining the list of allowed clients here, those that we let connect to the RADIUS server. If you go to the bottom of the list, going past the example settings, you will see the clients' secret has a default of testing123 – we want this changed to test.

7. Now we can use freeradius-wpe -s -X command to start the server. You will see a great many debug messages but, given time, it will settle down and start listening for the requests

Now we are ready to get down to work

Attacking PEAP

PEAP stands for Protected Extensible Authentication Protocol and is the most popular EAP version, shipped with Windows natively. There are two versions of PEAP:

- PEAPv0 with EAP-MSCHAPv2 – very popular as it has native Windows support

- PEAPv1 with EAP-GTC

To validate the RADIUS server, PEAP makes use of server-side certificates. Pretty much every PEAP attack makes use of the bad configuration in the validation of certificates.

Let's have a go at cracking PEAP:

1. First, make sure that PEAP is enabled – look in the eap.config file

2. The RADIUS server needs to be restarted using the command freeradius-wpe -s -X

3. Monitor the log file that FreeRADIUS-WPE created

4. Because Windows has got PEAP native support, we need to make sure that certificate verification has been disabled – go into Protected EAP Properties in your Windows settings and click the Configure tab (beside Secured Password (EAP-MSCHAP v2). Tell Windows that you do not want your Windows login credentials used automatically.

5. We must also force it into selecting User Authentication so click on the Advanced Settings box and select the option to Specify Authentication mode as User Authentication

6. As soon as the client makes a connection to the access point, a box appears asking for the login credentials. We have used a user name of Monster and a password of abcdefgh. Input these and look in the log file – the MSCHAP v2 challenge response will appear

7. Lastly, asleap is used to crack it through a password list containing an entry of abcdefgh – password successfully cracked

Security Best Practice

Far too many attacks have happened on WPA/WPA2, not just Enterprise but Personal too. Regardless of whether you are a personal or enterprise client, always use WPA2-PSK couple with a very strong passphrase – you are given 63 characters for this, use them!

If you are running a large business, set WPA2-Enterprise with EAP-TLS as this makes use of server and client-side certificates for authentication and, right now, it has yet to be hacked.

If you must use either PEAP or EAP-TLS when you are using WPA2-Enterprise, make sure that you have enabled certificate validation and that you choose the correct certifying authorities, you only use authorized RADIUS servers and lastly, any of the settings that let RADIUS servers, certifying authorities or certificates be accepted by a user are disabled.

Chapter 10:

WPS and Probes

In this penultimate chapter, we will be looking at some of the newer techniques in terms of WPS attacks and monitoring probes, and that includes the Pineapple tool that makes it much easier to test your wireless system.

WPS Attacks

WPS, or Wireless Protected Setup, was first brought out in 2006 as a way of providing users with little to no wireless knowledge a way of having a secure network. The idea behind it was that the Wi-Fi enabled device they were using would have one hidden value that was hardcoded; this value would allow access only with key memorization. Authentication of newer devices would be done by pressing a button on the wireless router. Anyone who did not have physical access to that device would not be granted access and that was, to all intents and purposes, the solution to the problems surrounding WPA keys – either having to remember what they were or setting shorter ones to make it easier.

This seemed to work just fine until 2011. At this point a vulnerability was disclosed and this vulnerability allowed for brute-force attacks on the authentication system. The traffic that was needed to get through a QPS exchange could be easily spoofed and the WPS pin was just 8 characters out of a possible 10, from 0 to 9. This allows for just 100,000,000 potential combinations and that might seem a lot – until you compare it to a password of 8 characters containing azAZ09 characters – that has 218,340,105,584,896 potential combinations.

There are more vulnerabilities than this, though.

Out of the 8 characters in the WPS pin, the last one is a checksum which verifies the other 7 and that makes it predictable. That knocks the number of combinations down to 10,000,000.

The first 4 characters are checked separately from the next 3, meaning there are 104 + 103 or 11,000 combinations.

See how the number is dropping?

From just 2 decisions in the authentication, the number of potential combinations has dropped from 100,000,000 to just 11,000 – in terms of a brute force attack, that's a reduction in 6 hours of time needed to break in and it's this that makes QPS attacks incredibly viable.

Next, we are going to identify a WPA setup with vulnerabilities and attack it with Wash and Reaver.

1. We can't attack an access point with WPS until we have created one. BY default the TP-Link router I've been using already has this enabled as a default ad while this is quite worrying it is also convenient. Check yours by logging onto your router and see what the security is – set it to WPS if needed.

2. Now we can set the target up along with the testing environments. For this we use a tool called Wash and to function, this needs a monitoring interface. We've done this many times already throughout the book so set it up using the command: airmon-ng start wlan0

3. Next, we can call Wash with the command: wash –i wlan0mon

4. You will see displayed on Wash all devices in range that have WPS support. You will also see whether each device has active or unlocked WPS and what version it is

5. You should see from the list that the Wireless Lab access point has support for WPS, is on v1 and is unlocked. That's great. Make a note of the MAC address – mine is E8:94:F6:62:1E:8E – as you will need this for targeting reaver, the next tool we use.

6. The reaver tool is used to try a brute-force attack on the WPS pin for a MAC address that is

specified. Input the following syntax to get this started: reaver -i wlan0mon -b <mac> -vv

7. It should confirm the MAC address that the attack is going to happen on

8. Once it begins, reaver goes through every combination possible for the WPS pin and tries to authenticate it. Once it has, it returns the code and the password

With WPA-PSK enabled now we can authenticate as we would normally My device has the default WPA-PSK matching the WPS pin but if you wanted the authentication done with the pin you would specify the following command (substituting my pin for your own):reaver -i wlan0mon -b <mac> -vv -p 88404148

Probe Sniffing

We talked about probes earlier and how to use them for identifying a hidden network and for performing rogue access point attacks. We can also use them to identify an individual as a target or, using the least amount of equipment, to track targets en-masse.

When a device wants to connect to a wireless network, it will send a probe out. That probe contains the device MAC and the network name that it wants to connect to. Tools such as airodump-ng can be used for tracking these, but if we wanted to see if an individual was at a given location at a given time, or if we wanted to identify Wi-Fi usage trends, we need to go down another route.

We're going to use tshark and Python for the collection of data.

- First, we want a device that can look for several networks; any smartphone will do the job – these are better than desktops for an obvious reason; smartphones are mobile, desktops aren't. However do check whether your newer mobile device has disabled probe requests – if it has, it won't work.

- Enable Wi-Fi on your mobile and then set up your monitoring interface – airmon-ng start wlan0

- Use tshark to look for probe requests using this command: tshark -n -i wlan0mon subtype probereq

- Right now, your output is going to look rough. This is because the tshark output isn't designed for easy reading, just to cram as much info as it can in. What you can see clearly is the probe request's MAC and SSID. We can make this output look better by using this command: tshark –n –i wlan0mon –T fields -e wlan.sa –e wlan.ssid

- That looks better so, what comes next? We now need a Python script to run our command and then record what the output is so we can analyze it later. Before you run the code, make sure your monitoring interface is ready and that you have a file named results.txt in the current directory. The Python script is:

```
import subprocess
import datetime
results = open("results.txt", "a")
while 1:
    cmd = subprocess.check_output(["tshark –n –i wlan0mon –T fields -e wlan.sa –e wlan.ssid –c 100"], shell=True)
    split = cmd.split("\n")
    for value in split[:-1]:
        if value.strip():
            splitvalue = value.split("\t")
            MAC = str(splitvalue[0])
            SSID = str(splitvalue[1])
            time = str(datetime.datetime.now())
            results.write(MAC+" "+SSID+" "+time+"\r\n")
```

Let's break this down:

import subprocess and import datetime: We use these to reference the libraries called subprocess and datetime. Subprocess lets us monitor our interface using the command line in Linus while datetime lets us obtain the correct data and time readings

results = open("results.txt," "a"): With this we are opening a file that has the append rights and then assigning it t results. The append rights let the script add to the file contents, nothing more – this means the file cannot be overwritten

while 1: This is saying that it will run until it is stopped

cmd = subprocess.check_output(["tshark –n –i wlan0mon –T fields -e wlan.sa –e wlan.ssid –c 100"], shell=True): A shell is opened so our previous tshark command can be performed. The difference here is the addition of -c 100. This flag limits our command to just 100 queries which, in turn, lets us return the results back to ourselves without the program having to be stopped. Because we indicated that the script should run forever once the results are written, it will start again. The line takes the shell output and assigns it to the variable called cmd. A count to 100 will be displayed by the script; it will stop and then it will start again so, if you want it to stop, the process must be killed.

split = cmd.split("\n"): The variable is split line by line

for value in split[:-1]: The following action is repeated for each of the output lines, ignoring the initial line with the headers

if value.strip(): A check is made on the value to see if it is empty before the script continues to account for requests that are not probes

value = value.split("\t"): Each line is broken down further into smaller pieces using a delimiter of the tab character

These 3 lines take each of the pieces of text and assign it to a specified variable:

1. MAC = str(splitvalue[0])

2. SSID = str(splitvalue[1])

3. time = str(datetime.datetime.now())

results.write(MAC+" "+SSID+" "+time+"\r\n"): All the values are written into a file, each separated with a space. A return and a new line keep things neat and the output will be tidy lines of text written into the file.

This takes all the values, writes them to a file separated by spaces, and ends with a return and a new line for neatness. The output will be neat lines of text written to the file.

That brings us to the end of this guide. At first glance it might look like all I've showed you is how to hack but, look carefully and you will see that you now have the tools at hand to test your own network and protect it from similar attacks.

Bonus Chapter:

Staying Safe Online

The last year has been pretty bad for hacking. We've all head the horror stories of people's information being stolen, of identity theft, data breaches, phishing scams, ransomware attacks and more. We've shown you how to use Kali to test your own system, to see what vulnerabilities exist and now you are prepared for the worst. Aren't you?

This is such a serious problem that a consortium of five of the largest countries has pushed out a report that tells us of the five most common hacking attacks and what you can do to protect your credentials and your ID. The two most frightening things about these attacks are that they are easy for a hacker to pull off and they can do it with free software.

RAT – Remote Access Trojans

These are scary attacks in which a hacker will use malware to gain remote access to your devices. The software they use is free and they can see exactly what you are doing, they install keyloggers so they can track your passwords and they can do all of this with one simple phishing scam on just about any device and any operating system.

Protecting yourself is quite straightforward. The main thing is reputable anti-virus software – a free one will do the job so long as it set to update automatically. Also update every program on your device and install all security patches as soon as they are released. Especially those for your operating system.

Web Shells

Web shells allow hackers to have remote access to your devices, allowing them to take over and do all sorts of things, including renaming your files.

Again, protection boils down to ensuring all software and your operating system are kept fully up to date with all security patches installed.

Credential Stealers

If you are a Windows users and you work over a home or office network, no doubt you have heard of something called MimiKatz. This is a credential stealer that allows a hacker to make use of LSASS (Local Security Authority Subsystem) on Windows to gain access to several network machines. This has been used in some ransomware attacks in which companies, government agencies and hospitals have paid to get their computer systems unlocked.

The easiest way to protect yourself is to ensure that Windows is fully up to date. If you are not sure, click on start>Update and Security>Check for Updates. You can also make use of security features like Credential Guard.

Lateral Movement Networks

Originally, PowerShell Empire, which is the lateral movement network, was designed as a tool for testing. They started out with the right intentions but have since been exploited by hackers who now use PowerShell Empire and other similar networks to navigate computer networks. They then use them to steal credentials and run malware attacks and, because they have been built using genuine tools, they are hard to detect and they can run in your computer memory.

Unless you are competent and confident, you should hire an IT professional to check your system for PowerShell activity that has been compromised. The first step is to delete the older versions. You should also restrict who can access PowerShell and monitor it very carefully for malicious activity

Obfuscation Tools

A hacker is a criminal who operates online and hide themselves from you. They keep their attacks hidden as well, but the consequences are grim – often your identity is stolen, your bank account cleaned out, your credit card details stolen and more. More often than not, they make use of obfuscation tools to stop themselves from being detected and they redirect transmissions to remote hosts using TCP or Transmission Control Protocol.

Some tools, such as HTran have to be installed on your laptop, which means the hacker needs physical access. To that end, good strong passwords are needed to lock your devices. This should be combined with a firewall, although most operating systems have one built-in. Do make sure it is enabled though!

With these steps, you should be able to keep yourself just that little bit safer. At the end of the day, it comes down to being diligent, maintaining updates on everything you use and using strong passwords – and not the same one for everything you use.

Conclusion

Thanks for taking the time to read my guide. We've taken things a bit further and have gone slightly more complex this time but, as you probably noticed, the basic premise of penetration testing to secure your own network is the same, whether you are a beginner, intermediate or more advanced learner.

Identity theft and data theft are all too common these days and protecting yourself from attack is of paramount importance. You can't do that unless you can understand the ways that a hacker will get into a system and you might just be surprised at how many open doors are on yours. We take it for granted that having a firewall and anti-virus software is enough but, as it's clear to see it isn't. Weak passwords, ineffectual anti-virus protection, firewalls that haven't been set up properly, all of these and more will open the doors to the hackers.

Learn how to protect your system now and keep yourself cocooned in a bubble of safety.

Thank you, once again, for taking the time to read this.

Download the Audio Book Version of the book Hacking With Kali Linux : A Comprehensive, Step-By-Step Beginner's Guide to Learn Ethical Hacking With

Practical Examples to Computer Hacking, Wireless Network, Cybersecurity and Penetration Testing

Start your free 30-day trial

- Free membership for 30 days with 1 audiobook + 2 Audible Originals.

- After trial, 3 titles each month: 1 audiobook + 2 Audible Originals.

- Roll over any unused credits for up to 5 months.

- Exclusive audio-guided wellness programs.

Visit the below audible website to get started!

Audible US

Audible UK

Audible FR

Audible DE

Will You Help Me?

Hi there, avid reader! If you have extra time on your hands, I would really, really appreciate it if you could take a moment to visit my author profile in Amazon. In there, you will find all the titles I authored and who knows, you might find more interesting topics to read and learn!

If it's not too much to ask, you can also leave and write a review for all the titles that you have read – whether it's a positive or negative review. An honest and constructive review of my titles is always welcome and appreciated since it will only help me moving forward in creating these books. There will always be room to add or improve, or sometimes even subtract certain topics, that is why these reviews are always important for us. They will also assist other avid readers, professionals who are looking to sharpen their knowledge, or even newbies to any topic, in their search for the book that caters to their needs the most.

If you don't want to leave a review yourself, you can also vote on the existing reviews by voting Helpful (Thumbs Up) or Unhelpful (Thumbs Down), especially on the top 10 or so reviews.

If you want to go directly to the vote or review process, just visit on any of the below titles:

Hacking With Kali Linux : A Comprehensive, Step-By-Step Beginner's Guide to Learn Ethical Hacking With Practical Examples to Computer Hacking, Wireless Network, Cybersecurity and Penetration Testing

Machine Learning For Beginners : A Comprehensive, Step-by-Step Guide to Learning and Understanding Machine Learning Concepts, Technology and Principles for Beginners

The Ultimate Excel VBA Master: A Complete, Step-by-Step Guide to Becoming Excel VBA Master from Scratch

Again, I truly appreciate the time and effort that you will be putting in leaving a review for my titles or even just for voting. This will only inspire me to create more quality content and titles in the future.

Thank you and have a great day!

Peter Bradley

Resources

https://www.kali.org/downloads/

https://www.informationsecuritybuzz.com

www.berghel.net/col-edit/security_wise/

https://www.hackingtutorials.org ›

https://null-byte.wonderhowto.com/

https://www.theguardian.com/.

https://searchnetworking.techtarget.com/.

https://www.cybrary.it/0p3n

https://www.darkreading.com

https://www.kalitutorials.net

https://opensource.com

https://www.juniper.net ›

https://medium.com/

https://www.blackhat.com/

https://www.greycampus.com

https://www.krackattacks.com/

https://www.tripwire.com

https://security.stackexchange.com

https://documentation.meraki.com

www.ingramcontent.com/pod-product-compliance
Lightning Source LLC
Chambersburg PA
CBHW072224170526
45158CB00002BA/731